Read Through the Bible in One Year

PROGRESS TRACKER & DAILY WORKBOOK

written & designed by Shalana Frisby

Get organized for success in your bible study.
Download your bonus free printables now:

WWW.123JOURNALIT.COM / FREEBIES

SCRIPTURE FLASHCARDS - BIBLE READING PROMPTS - JOURNALING PAGES

More information at: www.123journalit.com

First Printing: November 2018
1 2 3 Journal It Publishing

ISBN-13: 978-1-947209-94-7

Plan Record

NAME:

_____

_____

READING START DATE:

_____ / _____ / _____

DATE COMPLETED:

_____ / _____ / _____

BIBLE VERSION(S) USED TO READ:

_____

_____

_____

_____

_____

SOURCE OF BIBLE READING PLAN USED:

_____

_____

_____

_____

_____

Books of the Bible Checklist

OLD TESTAMENT

- ☐ GENESIS
- ☐ EXODUS
- ☐ LEVITICUS
- ☐ NUMBERS
- ☐ DEUTERONOMY
- ☐ JOSHUA
- ☐ JUDGES
- ☐ RUTH
- ☐ 1 SAMUEL
- ☐ 2 SAMUEL
- ☐ 1 KINGS
- ☐ 2 KINGS
- ☐ 1 CHRONICLES
- ☐ 2 CHRONICLES
- ☐ EZRA
- ☐ NEHEMIAH
- ☐ ESTHER
- ☐ JOB
- ☐ PSALMS
- ☐ PROVERBS
- ☐ ECCLESIASTES
- ☐ SONG OF SOLOMON
- ☐ ISAIAH
- ☐ JEREMIAH
- ☐ LAMENTATIONS
- ☐ EZEKIEL
- ☐ DANIEL
- ☐ HOSEA
- ☐ JOEL
- ☐ AMOS
- ☐ OBADIAH
- ☐ JONAH
- ☐ MICAH
- ☐ NAHUM
- ☐ HABAKKUK
- ☐ ZEPHANIAH
- ☐ HAGGAI
- ☐ ZECHARIAH
- ☐ MALACHI

NEW TESTAMENT

- ☐ MATTHEW
- ☐ MARK
- ☐ LUKE
- ☐ JOHN
- ☐ ACTS
- ☐ ROMANS
- ☐ 1 CORINTHIANS
- ☐ 2 CORINTHIANS
- ☐ GALATIANS
- ☐ EPHESIANS
- ☐ PHILIPPIANS
- ☐ COLOSSIANS
- ☐ 1 THESSALONIANS
- ☐ 2 THESSALONIANS
- ☐ 1 TIMOTHY
- ☐ 2 TIMOTHY
- ☐ TITUS
- ☐ PHILEMON
- ☐ HEBREWS
- ☐ JAMES
- ☐ 1 PETER
- ☐ 2 PETER
- ☐ 1 JOHN
- ☐ 2 JOHN
- ☐ 3 JOHN
- ☐ JUDE
- ☐ REVELATION

Monthly Bible Reading Plan

MONTH:		MONTH:		MONTH:	
DATE	BIBLE READING	DATE	BIBLE READING	DATE	BIBLE READING

Monthly Bible Reading Plan

MONTH:		MONTH:		MONTH:	
DATE	BIBLE READING	DATE	BIBLE READING	DATE	BIBLE READING

Monthly Bible Reading Plan

MONTH:			MONTH:			MONTH:	
DATE	**BIBLE READING**		**DATE**	**BIBLE READING**		**DATE**	**BIBLE READING**

Monthly Bible Reading Plan

MONTH:			MONTH:			MONTH:	
DATE	BIBLE READING		DATE	BIBLE READING		DATE	BIBLE READING

NOTES:

_____
_____
_____
_____
_____
_____
_____
_____
_____
_____
_____

FAVORITE VERSE:

_____
_____
_____
_____

Today's Date & Time:

____ / ____ / _____   ____ : ____

Bible Passages Read:

_____
_____
_____

Prayer Concerns & Praise:

_____
_____
_____
_____
_____
_____

NOTES:

_____
_____
_____
_____
_____
_____
_____
_____
_____
_____
_____

FAVORITE VERSE:

_____
_____
_____
_____

Today's Date & Time:

____ / ____ / _____   ____ : ____

Bible Passages Read:

_____
_____
_____

Prayer Concerns & Praise:

_____
_____
_____
_____
_____
_____

NOTES:

FAVORITE VERSE:

Today's Date & Time:

____ / ____ / ____   ____ : ____

Bible Passages Read:

Prayer Concerns & Praise:

NOTES:

FAVORITE VERSE:

Today's Date & Time:

____ / ____ / ____   ____ : ____

Bible Passages Read:

Prayer Concerns & Praise:

NOTES:

_____

_____

_____

_____

_____

_____

_____

_____

_____

_____

_____

_____

FAVORITE VERSE:

_____

_____

_____

Today's Date & Time:

____ / ____ / ____   ____ : ____

Bible Passages Read:

_____

_____

_____

Prayer Concerns & Praise:

_____

_____

_____

_____

_____

NOTES:

_____

_____

_____

_____

_____

_____

_____

_____

_____

_____

_____

_____

FAVORITE VERSE:

_____

_____

_____

Today's Date & Time:

____ / ____ / ____   ____ : ____

Bible Passages Read:

_____

_____

_____

Prayer Concerns & Praise:

_____

_____

_____

_____

_____

NOTES:

FAVORITE VERSE:

Today's Date & Time:

____ / ____ / ____   ____ : ____

Bible Passages Read:

Prayer Concerns & Praise:

NOTES:

FAVORITE VERSE:

Today's Date & Time:

____ / ____ / ____   ____ : ____

Bible Passages Read:

Prayer Concerns & Praise:

NOTES: _____

_____
_____
_____
_____
_____
_____
_____
_____
_____
_____
_____
_____

FAVORITE VERSE:

_____
_____
_____

Today's Date & Time:

____ / ____ / _____   ____ : ____

Bible Passages Read:

_____
_____
_____

Prayer Concerns & Praise:

_____
_____
_____
_____
_____

NOTES: _____

_____
_____
_____
_____
_____
_____
_____
_____
_____
_____
_____
_____

FAVORITE VERSE:

_____
_____
_____

Today's Date & Time:

____ / ____ / _____   ____ : ____

Bible Passages Read:

_____
_____
_____

Prayer Concerns & Praise:

_____
_____
_____
_____
_____

NOTES:

FAVORITE VERSE:

Today's Date & Time:

____ / ____ / ____   ____ : ____

Bible Passages Read:

Prayer Concerns & Praise:

NOTES:

FAVORITE VERSE:

Today's Date & Time:

____ / ____ / ____   ____ : ____

Bible Passages Read:

Prayer Concerns & Praise:

NOTES:

FAVORITE VERSE:

Today's Date & Time:

____ / ____ / ____   ____ : ____

Bible Passages Read:

Prayer Concerns & Praise:

NOTES:

FAVORITE VERSE:

Today's Date & Time:

____ / ____ / ____   ____ : ____

Bible Passages Read:

Prayer Concerns & Praise:

NOTES:

FAVORITE VERSE:

NOTES:

FAVORITE VERSE:

Today's Date & Time:

___ / ___ / _____   ____ : ____

Bible Passages Read:

Prayer Concerns & Praise:

Today's Date & Time:

___ / ___ / _____   ____ : ____

Bible Passages Read:

Prayer Concerns & Praise:

NOTES: _____

_____
_____
_____
_____
_____
_____
_____
_____
_____
_____
_____

FAVORITE VERSE:

_____
_____
_____

Today's Date & Time:

____ / ____ / ____   ____ : ____

Bible Passages Read:

_____
_____
_____

Prayer Concerns & Praise:

_____
_____
_____
_____
_____
_____

NOTES: _____

_____
_____
_____
_____
_____
_____
_____
_____
_____
_____

FAVORITE VERSE:

_____
_____
_____

Today's Date & Time:

____ / ____ / ____   ____ : ____

Bible Passages Read:

_____
_____
_____

Prayer Concerns & Praise:

_____
_____
_____
_____
_____
_____

NOTES:

FAVORITE VERSE:

Today's Date & Time:

_____ / _____ / _____   _____ : _____

Bible Passages Read:

Prayer Concerns & Praise:

NOTES:

FAVORITE VERSE:

Today's Date & Time:

_____ / _____ / _____   _____ : _____

Bible Passages Read:

Prayer Concerns & Praise:

NOTES: _____

_____
_____
_____
_____
_____
_____
_____
_____
_____
_____
_____
_____

FAVORITE VERSE: _____

_____
_____
_____

Today's Date & Time:

____ / ____ / ____   ____ : ____

Bible Passages Read:

_____
_____

Prayer Concerns & Praise:

_____
_____
_____
_____
_____

NOTES: _____

_____
_____
_____
_____
_____
_____
_____
_____
_____
_____

FAVORITE VERSE: _____

_____
_____
_____

Today's Date & Time:

____ / ____ / ____   ____ : ____

Bible Passages Read:

_____
_____

Prayer Concerns & Praise:

_____
_____
_____
_____
_____

NOTES:

FAVORITE VERSE:

NOTES:

FAVORITE VERSE:

Today's Date & Time:

____ / ____ / ____   ____ : ____

Bible Passages Read:

Prayer Concerns & Praise:

Today's Date & Time:

____ / ____ / ____   ____ : ____

Bible Passages Read:

Prayer Concerns & Praise:

22

NOTES:

FAVORITE VERSE:

Today's Date & Time:

____ / ____ / ____   ____ : ____

Bible Passages Read:

Prayer Concerns & Praise:

NOTES:

FAVORITE VERSE:

Today's Date & Time:

____ / ____ / ____   ____ : ____

Bible Passages Read:

Prayer Concerns & Praise:

NOTES:

_____
_____
_____
_____
_____
_____
_____
_____
_____
_____
_____

FAVORITE VERSE:

_____
_____
_____
_____

Today's Date & Time:

____ / ____ / ____   ____ : ____

Bible Passages Read:

_____
_____
_____

Prayer Concerns & Praise:

_____
_____
_____
_____
_____
_____
_____

NOTES:

_____
_____
_____
_____
_____
_____
_____
_____
_____
_____
_____

FAVORITE VERSE:

_____
_____
_____
_____

Today's Date & Time:

____ / ____ / ____   ____ : ____

Bible Passages Read:

_____
_____
_____

Prayer Concerns & Praise:

_____
_____
_____
_____
_____

NOTES: _____

_____

_____

_____

_____

_____

_____

_____

_____

_____

_____

FAVORITE VERSE:

_____

_____

_____

Today's Date & Time:

____ / ____ / _____   ____ : ____

Bible Passages Read:

_____

_____

_____

Prayer Concerns & Praise:

_____

_____

_____

_____

_____

NOTES: _____

_____

_____

_____

_____

_____

_____

_____

_____

_____

_____

FAVORITE VERSE:

_____

_____

_____

Today's Date & Time:

____ / ____ / _____   ____ : ____

Bible Passages Read:

_____

_____

_____

Prayer Concerns & Praise:

_____

_____

_____

_____

_____

NOTES:

FAVORITE VERSE:

Today's Date & Time:

___ / ___ / _____   ____ : ____

Bible Passages Read:

Prayer Concerns & Praise:

NOTES:

FAVORITE VERSE:

Today's Date & Time:

___ / ___ / _____   ____ : ____

Bible Passages Read:

Prayer Concerns & Praise:

NOTES:

FAVORITE VERSE:

Today's Date & Time:

_____ / _____ / _____   _____ : _____

Bible Passages Read:

Prayer Concerns & Praise:

NOTES:

FAVORITE VERSE:

Today's Date & Time:

_____ / _____ / _____   _____ : _____

Bible Passages Read:

Prayer Concerns & Praise:

NOTES: _____

_____
_____
_____
_____
_____
_____
_____
_____
_____
_____
_____

FAVORITE VERSE:

_____
_____
_____

NOTES: _____

_____
_____
_____
_____
_____
_____
_____
_____
_____
_____
_____

FAVORITE VERSE:

_____
_____
_____

Today's Date & Time:

_____ / _____ / _____   _____ : _____

Bible Passages Read:

_____
_____

Prayer Concerns & Praise:

_____
_____
_____
_____
_____

Today's Date & Time:

_____ / _____ / _____   _____ : _____

Bible Passages Read:

_____
_____

Prayer Concerns & Praise:

_____
_____
_____
_____

NOTES: _____

_____
_____
_____
_____
_____
_____
_____
_____
_____
_____

FAVORITE VERSE:

_____
_____
_____
_____

Today's Date & Time:

____ / ____ / _____   ____ : ____

Bible Passages Read:

_____
_____
_____

Prayer Concerns & Praise:

_____
_____
_____
_____
_____
_____

NOTES: _____

_____
_____
_____
_____
_____
_____
_____
_____
_____
_____

FAVORITE VERSE:

_____
_____
_____
_____

Today's Date & Time:

____ / ____ / _____   ____ : ____

Bible Passages Read:

_____
_____
_____

Prayer Concerns & Praise:

_____
_____
_____
_____
_____
_____

NOTES:

_____

_____

_____

_____

_____

_____

_____

_____

_____

_____

_____

_____

_____

FAVORITE VERSE:

_____

_____

_____

Today's Date & Time:

____ / ____ / ____   ____ : ____

Bible Passages Read:

_____

_____

Prayer Concerns & Praise:

_____

_____

_____

_____

_____

NOTES:

_____

_____

_____

_____

_____

_____

_____

_____

_____

_____

_____

_____

_____

FAVORITE VERSE:

_____

_____

_____

Today's Date & Time:

____ / ____ / ____   ____ : ____

Bible Passages Read:

_____

_____

Prayer Concerns & Praise:

_____

_____

_____

_____

NOTES:

FAVORITE VERSE:

Today's Date & Time:

____ / ____ / ____   ____ : ____

Bible Passages Read:

Prayer Concerns & Praise:

NOTES:

FAVORITE VERSE:

Today's Date & Time:

____ / ____ / ____   ____ : ____

Bible Passages Read:

Prayer Concerns & Praise:

NOTES: _____

_____
_____
_____
_____
_____
_____
_____
_____
_____
_____
_____
_____

FAVORITE VERSE: _____

_____
_____
_____
_____

Today's Date & Time:

____ / ____ / ____   ____ : ____

Bible Passages Read:

_____
_____
_____

Prayer Concerns & Praise:

_____
_____
_____
_____
_____
_____

NOTES: _____

_____
_____
_____
_____
_____
_____
_____
_____
_____
_____
_____
_____

FAVORITE VERSE: _____

_____
_____
_____
_____

Today's Date & Time:

____ / ____ / ____   ____ : ____

Bible Passages Read:

_____
_____
_____

Prayer Concerns & Praise:

_____
_____
_____
_____
_____
_____

NOTES:

FAVORITE VERSE:

Today's Date & Time:

____ / ____ / _____   ____ : ____

Bible Passages Read:

Prayer Concerns & Praise:

NOTES:

FAVORITE VERSE:

Today's Date & Time:

____ / ____ / _____   ____ : ____

Bible Passages Read:

Prayer Concerns & Praise:

NOTES:

FAVORITE VERSE:

Today's Date & Time:

_____ / _____ / _____   _____ : _____

Bible Passages Read:

Prayer Concerns & Praise:

NOTES:

FAVORITE VERSE:

Today's Date & Time:

_____ / _____ / _____   _____ : _____

Bible Passages Read:

Prayer Concerns & Praise:

NOTES: _____

_____
_____
_____
_____
_____
_____
_____
_____
_____
_____
_____
_____

FAVORITE VERSE:

_____
_____
_____

Today's Date & Time:

____ / ____ / _____   ____ : ____

Bible Passages Read:

_____
_____

Prayer Concerns & Praise:

_____
_____
_____
_____
_____

NOTES: _____

_____
_____
_____
_____
_____
_____
_____
_____
_____
_____
_____

FAVORITE VERSE:

_____
_____
_____

Today's Date & Time:

____ / ____ / _____   ____ : ____

Bible Passages Read:

_____
_____

Prayer Concerns & Praise:

_____
_____
_____
_____
_____

NOTES:

FAVORITE VERSE:

Today's Date & Time:

____ / ____ / ____   ____ : ____

Bible Passages Read:

Prayer Concerns & Praise:

NOTES:

FAVORITE VERSE:

Today's Date & Time:

____ / ____ / ____   ____ : ____

Bible Passages Read:

Prayer Concerns & Praise:

NOTES:

FAVORITE VERSE:

Today's Date & Time:

____ / ____ / _____   ____ : ____

Bible Passages Read:

Prayer Concerns & Praise:

NOTES:

FAVORITE VERSE:

Today's Date & Time:

____ / ____ / _____   ____ : ____

Bible Passages Read:

Prayer Concerns & Praise:

NOTES:

FAVORITE VERSE:

Today's Date & Time:

_____ / _____ / _____   _____ : _____

Bible Passages Read:

Prayer Concerns & Praise:

NOTES:

FAVORITE VERSE:

Today's Date & Time:

_____ / _____ / _____   _____ : _____

Bible Passages Read:

Prayer Concerns & Praise:

NOTES: _____

_____
_____
_____
_____
_____
_____
_____
_____
_____
_____

FAVORITE VERSE: _____

_____
_____
_____

Today's Date & Time:

____ / ____ / ____   ____ : ____

Bible Passages Read:

_____
_____
_____

Prayer Concerns & Praise:

_____
_____
_____
_____
_____

NOTES: _____

_____
_____
_____
_____
_____
_____
_____
_____
_____
_____

FAVORITE VERSE: _____

_____
_____
_____

Today's Date & Time:

____ / ____ / ____   ____ : ____

Bible Passages Read:

_____
_____
_____

Prayer Concerns & Praise:

_____
_____
_____
_____
_____

NOTES: _____

_____
_____
_____
_____
_____
_____
_____
_____
_____

FAVORITE VERSE:
_____
_____
_____

Today's Date & Time:

____ / ____ / _____   ____ : ____

Bible Passages Read:

_____
_____

Prayer Concerns & Praise:

_____
_____
_____
_____
_____

NOTES: _____

_____
_____
_____
_____
_____
_____
_____
_____
_____

FAVORITE VERSE:
_____
_____
_____

Today's Date & Time:

____ / ____ / _____   ____ : ____

Bible Passages Read:

_____
_____

Prayer Concerns & Praise:

_____
_____
_____
_____

NOTES:

FAVORITE VERSE:

Today's Date & Time:

____ / ____ / ____   ____ : ____

Bible Passages Read:

Prayer Concerns & Praise:

NOTES:

FAVORITE VERSE:

Today's Date & Time:

____ / ____ / ____   ____ : ____

Bible Passages Read:

Prayer Concerns & Praise:

NOTES: _____

_____

_____

_____

_____

_____

_____

_____

_____

_____

_____

FAVORITE VERSE:

_____

_____

_____

Today's Date & Time:

____ / ____ / ____   ____ : ____

Bible Passages Read:

_____

_____

Prayer Concerns & Praise:

_____

_____

_____

_____

_____

NOTES: _____

_____

_____

_____

_____

_____

_____

_____

_____

_____

_____

FAVORITE VERSE:

_____

_____

_____

Today's Date & Time:

____ / ____ / ____   ____ : ____

Bible Passages Read:

_____

_____

Prayer Concerns & Praise:

_____

_____

_____

_____

NOTES: _____

_____
_____
_____
_____
_____
_____
_____
_____
_____
_____

FAVORITE VERSE:

_____
_____
_____
_____

Today's Date & Time:

____ / ____ / _____   ____ : ____

Bible Passages Read:

_____
_____
_____

Prayer Concerns & Praise:

_____
_____
_____
_____
_____

NOTES: _____

_____
_____
_____
_____
_____
_____
_____
_____
_____
_____

FAVORITE VERSE:

_____
_____
_____
_____

Today's Date & Time:

____ / ____ / _____   ____ : ____

Bible Passages Read:

_____
_____
_____

Prayer Concerns & Praise:

_____
_____
_____
_____
_____

NOTES: _____

_____
_____
_____
_____
_____
_____
_____
_____
_____
_____
_____

FAVORITE VERSE: _____

_____
_____
_____

Today's Date & Time:

____ / ____ / _____   ____ : ____

Bible Passages Read:

_____
_____
_____

Prayer Concerns & Praise:

_____
_____
_____
_____
_____
_____

NOTES: _____

_____
_____
_____
_____
_____
_____
_____
_____
_____
_____
_____

FAVORITE VERSE: _____

_____
_____
_____

Today's Date & Time:

____ / ____ / _____   ____ : ____

Bible Passages Read:

_____
_____
_____

Prayer Concerns & Praise:

_____
_____
_____
_____
_____

NOTES:

FAVORITE VERSE:

Today's Date & Time:

___ / ___ / ___   ___ : ___

Bible Passages Read:

Prayer Concerns & Praise:

NOTES:

FAVORITE VERSE:

Today's Date & Time:

___ / ___ / ___   ___ : ___

Bible Passages Read:

Prayer Concerns & Praise:

NOTES:

FAVORITE VERSE:

Today's Date & Time:

___ / ___ / _____   ___ : _____

Bible Passages Read:

Prayer Concerns & Praise:

NOTES:

FAVORITE VERSE:

Today's Date & Time:

___ / ___ / _____   ___ : _____

Bible Passages Read:

Prayer Concerns & Praise:

NOTES: _____

_____

_____

_____

_____

_____

_____

_____

_____

_____

_____

_____

FAVORITE VERSE: _____

_____

_____

_____

Today's Date & Time:

____ / ____ / _____   _____ : ____

Bible Passages Read:

_____

_____

_____

Prayer Concerns & Praise:

_____

_____

_____

_____

_____

NOTES: _____

_____

_____

_____

_____

_____

_____

_____

_____

_____

_____

_____

FAVORITE VERSE: _____

_____

_____

_____

Today's Date & Time:

____ / ____ / _____   _____ : ____

Bible Passages Read:

_____

_____

_____

Prayer Concerns & Praise:

_____

_____

_____

_____

_____

NOTES: _____

_____
_____
_____
_____
_____
_____
_____
_____
_____
_____
_____

FAVORITE VERSE: _____

_____
_____
_____

Today's Date & Time:

____ / ____ / ____   ____ : ____

Bible Passages Read:

_____
_____

Prayer Concerns & Praise:

_____
_____
_____
_____
_____

NOTES: _____

_____
_____
_____
_____
_____
_____
_____
_____
_____
_____
_____

FAVORITE VERSE: _____

_____
_____
_____

Today's Date & Time:

____ / ____ / ____   ____ : ____

Bible Passages Read:

_____
_____

Prayer Concerns & Praise:

_____
_____
_____
_____
_____

NOTES: _____

_____
_____
_____
_____
_____
_____
_____
_____
_____
_____
_____

FAVORITE VERSE:

_____
_____
_____

Today's Date & Time:

____ / ____ / _____   ____ : ____

Bible Passages Read:

_____
_____
_____

Prayer Concerns & Praise:

_____
_____
_____
_____
_____
_____

NOTES: _____

_____
_____
_____
_____
_____
_____
_____
_____
_____
_____
_____

FAVORITE VERSE:

_____
_____
_____

Today's Date & Time:

____ / ____ / _____   ____ : ____

Bible Passages Read:

_____
_____
_____

Prayer Concerns & Praise:

_____
_____
_____
_____
_____

NOTES: _____

_____

_____

_____

_____

_____

_____

_____

_____

_____

_____

FAVORITE VERSE: _____

_____

_____

_____

Today's Date & Time:

____ / ____ / _____   ____ : ____

Bible Passages Read:

_____

_____

_____

Prayer Concerns & Praise:

_____

_____

_____

_____

_____

NOTES: _____

_____

_____

_____

_____

_____

_____

_____

_____

_____

_____

_____

FAVORITE VERSE: _____

_____

_____

_____

Today's Date & Time:

____ / ____ / _____   ____ : ____

Bible Passages Read:

_____

_____

_____

Prayer Concerns & Praise:

_____

_____

_____

_____

_____

NOTES: _____

_____

_____

_____

_____

_____

_____

_____

_____

_____

_____

_____

FAVORITE VERSE:

_____

_____

_____

Today's Date & Time:

_____ / _____ / _____   _____ : _____

Bible Passages Read:

_____

_____

_____

Prayer Concerns & Praise:

_____

_____

_____

_____

_____

NOTES: _____

_____

_____

_____

_____

_____

_____

_____

_____

_____

_____

_____

FAVORITE VERSE:

_____

_____

_____

Today's Date & Time:

_____ / _____ / _____   _____ : _____

Bible Passages Read:

_____

_____

_____

Prayer Concerns & Praise:

_____

_____

_____

_____

_____

NOTES: _____

_____
_____
_____
_____
_____
_____
_____
_____
_____
_____
_____

FAVORITE VERSE:

_____
_____
_____

Today's Date & Time:

____ / ____ / ____   ____ : ____

Bible Passages Read:

_____
_____

Prayer Concerns & Praise:

_____
_____
_____
_____
_____

NOTES: _____

_____
_____
_____
_____
_____
_____
_____
_____
_____
_____
_____

FAVORITE VERSE:

_____
_____
_____

Today's Date & Time:

____ / ____ / ____   ____ : ____

Bible Passages Read:

_____
_____

Prayer Concerns & Praise:

_____
_____
_____
_____
_____

NOTES:

FAVORITE VERSE:

Today's Date & Time:

_____ / _____ / _____   _____ : _____

Bible Passages Read:

Prayer Concerns & Praise:

NOTES:

FAVORITE VERSE:

Today's Date & Time:

_____ / _____ / _____   _____ : _____

Bible Passages Read:

Prayer Concerns & Praise:

NOTES:

_____

Today's Date & Time:

_____ / _____ / _____   _____ : _____

Bible Passages Read:

_____

_____

Prayer Concerns & Praise:

_____

_____

_____

_____

_____

FAVORITE VERSE:

_____

_____

NOTES:

_____

Today's Date & Time:

_____ / _____ / _____   _____ : _____

Bible Passages Read:

_____

_____

Prayer Concerns & Praise:

_____

_____

_____

_____

FAVORITE VERSE:

_____

_____

NOTES: _____

_____
_____
_____
_____
_____
_____
_____
_____
_____
_____
_____
_____

FAVORITE VERSE: _____

_____
_____
_____

Today's Date & Time:

____ / ____ / _____   ____ : ____

Bible Passages Read:

_____
_____
_____

Prayer Concerns & Praise:

_____
_____
_____
_____
_____
_____

NOTES: _____

_____
_____
_____
_____
_____
_____
_____
_____
_____
_____
_____
_____

FAVORITE VERSE: _____

_____
_____
_____

Today's Date & Time:

____ / ____ / _____   ____ : ____

Bible Passages Read:

_____
_____
_____

Prayer Concerns & Praise:

_____
_____
_____
_____
_____
_____

NOTES:

FAVORITE VERSE:

Today's Date & Time:

____ / ____ / _____   ____ : ____

Bible Passages Read:

Prayer Concerns & Praise:

NOTES:

FAVORITE VERSE:

Today's Date & Time:

____ / ____ / _____   ____ : ____

Bible Passages Read:

Prayer Concerns & Praise:

NOTES:

FAVORITE VERSE:

Today's Date & Time:

_____ / _____ / _____   _____ : _____

Bible Passages Read:

Prayer Concerns & Praise:

NOTES:

FAVORITE VERSE:

Today's Date & Time:

_____ / _____ / _____   _____ : _____

Bible Passages Read:

Prayer Concerns & Praise:

NOTES:

FAVORITE VERSE:

Today's Date & Time:

_____ / _____ / _____   _____ : _____

Bible Passages Read:

Prayer Concerns & Praise:

NOTES:

FAVORITE VERSE:

Today's Date & Time:

_____ / _____ / _____   _____ : _____

Bible Passages Read:

Prayer Concerns & Praise:

NOTES: _____

_____
_____
_____
_____
_____
_____
_____
_____
_____
_____
_____

FAVORITE VERSE:

_____
_____
_____
_____

Today's Date & Time:

____ / ____ / ____   ____ : ____

Bible Passages Read:

_____
_____
_____

Prayer Concerns & Praise:

_____
_____
_____
_____
_____

NOTES: _____

_____
_____
_____
_____
_____
_____
_____
_____
_____
_____
_____
_____

FAVORITE VERSE:

_____
_____
_____
_____

Today's Date & Time:

____ / ____ / ____   ____ : ____

Bible Passages Read:

_____
_____
_____

Prayer Concerns & Praise:

_____
_____
_____
_____
_____

NOTES:

FAVORITE VERSE:

Today's Date & Time:

____ / ____ / _____   ____ : ____

Bible Passages Read:

Prayer Concerns & Praise:

NOTES:

FAVORITE VERSE:

Today's Date & Time:

____ / ____ / _____   ____ : ____

Bible Passages Read:

Prayer Concerns & Praise:

NOTES:

FAVORITE VERSE:

Today's Date & Time:

____ / ____ / ____   ____ : ____

Bible Passages Read:

Prayer Concerns & Praise:

NOTES:

FAVORITE VERSE:

Today's Date & Time:

____ / ____ / ____   ____ : ____

Bible Passages Read:

Prayer Concerns & Praise:

NOTES: _____

_____
_____
_____
_____
_____
_____
_____
_____
_____
_____
_____

FAVORITE VERSE:

_____
_____
_____

Today's Date & Time:

_____ / _____ / _____   _____ : _____

Bible Passages Read:

_____
_____
_____

Prayer Concerns & Praise:

_____
_____
_____
_____
_____
_____

NOTES: _____

_____
_____
_____
_____
_____
_____
_____
_____
_____
_____
_____

FAVORITE VERSE:

_____
_____
_____

Today's Date & Time:

_____ / _____ / _____   _____ : _____

Bible Passages Read:

_____
_____
_____

Prayer Concerns & Praise:

_____
_____
_____
_____
_____
_____

NOTES:

FAVORITE VERSE:

Today's Date & Time:

____ / ____ / _____   ____ : ____

Bible Passages Read:

Prayer Concerns & Praise:

NOTES:

FAVORITE VERSE:

Today's Date & Time:

____ / ____ / _____   ____ : ____

Bible Passages Read:

Prayer Concerns & Praise:

NOTES:

FAVORITE VERSE:

Today's Date & Time:

____ / ____ / ____   ____ : ____

Bible Passages Read:

Prayer Concerns & Praise:

NOTES:

FAVORITE VERSE:

Today's Date & Time:

____ / ____ / ____   ____ : ____

Bible Passages Read:

Prayer Concerns & Praise:

NOTES:

FAVORITE VERSE:

Today's Date & Time:

___ / ___ / _____ ___ : ___

Bible Passages Read:

Prayer Concerns & Praise:

NOTES:

FAVORITE VERSE:

Today's Date & Time:

___ / ___ / _____ ___ : ___

Bible Passages Read:

Prayer Concerns & Praise:

NOTES: _____

_____

____ / ____ / ____   ____ : ____

Bible Passages Read:

_____

_____

Prayer Concerns & Praise:

_____

_____

_____

_____

_____

FAVORITE VERSE:

_____

_____

_____

NOTES: _____

_____

Today's Date & Time:

____ / ____ / ____   ____ : ____

Bible Passages Read:

_____

_____

Prayer Concerns & Praise:

_____

_____

_____

_____

FAVORITE VERSE:

_____

_____

_____

NOTES: _____

_____

_____

_____

_____

_____

_____

_____

_____

_____

_____

_____

FAVORITE VERSE:

_____

_____

_____

Today's Date & Time:

____ / ____ / ____   ____ : ____

Bible Passages Read:

_____

_____

_____

Prayer Concerns & Praise:

_____

_____

_____

_____

_____

NOTES: _____

_____

_____

_____

_____

_____

_____

_____

_____

_____

_____

_____

FAVORITE VERSE:

_____

_____

_____

Today's Date & Time:

____ / ____ / ____   ____ : ____

Bible Passages Read:

_____

_____

_____

Prayer Concerns & Praise:

_____

_____

_____

_____

_____

NOTES: _____

_____
_____
_____
_____
_____
_____
_____
_____
_____
_____

FAVORITE VERSE: _____

_____
_____
_____

Today's Date & Time:

____ / ____ / _____   ____ : ____

Bible Passages Read:

_____
_____
_____

Prayer Concerns & Praise:

_____
_____
_____
_____
_____
_____

NOTES: _____

_____
_____
_____
_____
_____
_____
_____
_____
_____
_____

FAVORITE VERSE: _____

_____
_____
_____

Today's Date & Time:

____ / ____ / _____   ____ : ____

Bible Passages Read:

_____
_____
_____

Prayer Concerns & Praise:

_____
_____
_____
_____
_____
_____

NOTES: _____

_____

_____

_____

_____

_____

_____

_____

_____

_____

_____

_____

FAVORITE VERSE:

_____

_____

_____

Today's Date & Time:

____ / ____ / _____   ____ : ____

Bible Passages Read:

_____

_____

_____

Prayer Concerns & Praise:

_____

_____

_____

_____

_____

NOTES: _____

_____

_____

_____

_____

_____

_____

_____

_____

_____

_____

_____

FAVORITE VERSE:

_____

_____

_____

Today's Date & Time:

____ / ____ / _____   ____ : ____

Bible Passages Read:

_____

_____

_____

Prayer Concerns & Praise:

_____

_____

_____

_____

_____

NOTES: _____

_____

_____

_____

_____

_____

_____

_____

_____

_____

_____

FAVORITE VERSE:

_____

_____

_____

Today's Date & Time:

____ / ____ / _____   ____ : ____

Bible Passages Read:

_____

_____

Prayer Concerns & Praise:

_____

_____

_____

_____

_____

NOTES: _____

_____

_____

_____

_____

_____

_____

_____

_____

_____

_____

FAVORITE VERSE:

_____

_____

_____

Today's Date & Time:

____ / ____ / _____   ____ : ____

Bible Passages Read:

_____

_____

Prayer Concerns & Praise:

_____

_____

_____

_____

NOTES: _____

_____
_____
_____
_____
_____
_____
_____
_____
_____
_____
_____

FAVORITE VERSE: _____

_____
_____
_____

Today's Date & Time:

____ / ____ / ____   ____ : ____

Bible Passages Read:

_____
_____
_____

Prayer Concerns & Praise:

_____
_____
_____
_____
_____
_____

NOTES: _____

_____
_____
_____
_____
_____
_____
_____
_____
_____
_____
_____

FAVORITE VERSE: _____

_____
_____
_____

Today's Date & Time:

____ / ____ / ____   ____ : ____

Bible Passages Read:

_____
_____
_____

Prayer Concerns & Praise:

_____
_____
_____
_____
_____
_____

NOTES:

FAVORITE VERSE:

Today's Date & Time:

____ / ____ / _____   ____ : ____

Bible Passages Read:

Prayer Concerns & Praise:

NOTES:

FAVORITE VERSE:

Today's Date & Time:

____ / ____ / _____   ____ : ____

Bible Passages Read:

Prayer Concerns & Praise:

NOTES:

FAVORITE VERSE:

Today's Date & Time:

____ / ____ / ____   ____ : ____

Bible Passages Read:

Prayer Concerns & Praise:

NOTES:

FAVORITE VERSE:

Today's Date & Time:

____ / ____ / ____   ____ : ____

Bible Passages Read:

Prayer Concerns & Praise:

NOTES:

_____

FAVORITE VERSE:

Today's Date & Time:

____ / ____ / ____   ____ : ____

Bible Passages Read:

Prayer Concerns & Praise:

NOTES:

FAVORITE VERSE:

Today's Date & Time:

____ / ____ / ____   ____ : ____

Bible Passages Read:

Prayer Concerns & Praise:

NOTES:

FAVORITE VERSE:

Today's Date & Time:

_____ / _____ / _____   _____ : _____

Bible Passages Read:

Prayer Concerns & Praise:

NOTES:

FAVORITE VERSE:

Today's Date & Time:

_____ / _____ / _____   _____ : _____

Bible Passages Read:

Prayer Concerns & Praise:

NOTES:

_____

_____

_____

_____

_____

_____

_____

_____

_____

_____

FAVORITE VERSE:

_____

_____

_____

Today's Date & Time:

____ / ____ / ____   ____ : ____

Bible Passages Read:

_____

_____

Prayer Concerns & Praise:

_____

_____

_____

_____

_____

NOTES:

_____

_____

_____

_____

_____

_____

_____

_____

_____

_____

FAVORITE VERSE:

_____

_____

_____

Today's Date & Time:

____ / ____ / ____   ____ : ____

Bible Passages Read:

_____

_____

Prayer Concerns & Praise:

_____

_____

_____

_____

NOTES:

FAVORITE VERSE:

NOTES:

FAVORITE VERSE:

Today's Date & Time:

____ / ____ / ____   ____ : ____

Bible Passages Read:

Prayer Concerns & Praise:

Today's Date & Time:

____ / ____ / ____   ____ : ____

Bible Passages Read:

Prayer Concerns & Praise:

NOTES:

_____
_____
_____
_____
_____
_____
_____
_____
_____
_____
_____

FAVORITE VERSE:

_____
_____
_____

Today's Date & Time:

____ / ____ / ____   ____ : ____

Bible Passages Read:

_____
_____
_____

Prayer Concerns & Praise:

_____
_____
_____
_____
_____
_____

NOTES:

_____
_____
_____
_____
_____
_____
_____
_____
_____
_____
_____

FAVORITE VERSE:

_____
_____
_____

Today's Date & Time:

____ / ____ / ____   ____ : ____

Bible Passages Read:

_____
_____
_____

Prayer Concerns & Praise:

_____
_____
_____
_____
_____

NOTES: _____

_____

_____

_____

_____

_____

_____

_____

_____

_____

_____

_____

FAVORITE VERSE:

_____

_____

_____

Today's Date & Time:

_____ / _____ / _____   _____ : _____

Bible Passages Read:

_____

_____

_____

Prayer Concerns & Praise:

_____

_____

_____

_____

_____

NOTES: _____

_____

_____

_____

_____

_____

_____

_____

_____

_____

_____

_____

FAVORITE VERSE:

_____

_____

_____

Today's Date & Time:

_____ / _____ / _____   _____ : _____

Bible Passages Read:

_____

_____

_____

Prayer Concerns & Praise:

_____

_____

_____

_____

_____

NOTES:

FAVORITE VERSE:

Today's Date & Time:

____ / ____ / ____   ____ : ____

Bible Passages Read:

Prayer Concerns & Praise:

NOTES:

FAVORITE VERSE:

Today's Date & Time:

____ / ____ / ____   ____ : ____

Bible Passages Read:

Prayer Concerns & Praise:

NOTES:

FAVORITE VERSE:

Today's Date & Time:

____ / ____ / _____   ____ : ____

Bible Passages Read:

Prayer Concerns & Praise:

NOTES:

FAVORITE VERSE:

Today's Date & Time:

____ / ____ / _____   ____ : ____

Bible Passages Read:

Prayer Concerns & Praise:

NOTES:

FAVORITE VERSE:

Today's Date & Time:

_____ / _____ / _____   _____ : _____

Bible Passages Read:

Prayer Concerns & Praise:

NOTES:

FAVORITE VERSE:

Today's Date & Time:

_____ / _____ / _____   _____ : _____

Bible Passages Read:

Prayer Concerns & Praise:

NOTES: _____

_____
_____
_____
_____
_____
_____
_____
_____
_____
_____
_____
_____
_____

FAVORITE VERSE:
_____
_____
_____
_____

Today's Date & Time:

___ / ___ / ____   ____ : ____

Bible Passages Read:

_____
_____
_____

Prayer Concerns & Praise:

_____
_____
_____
_____
_____

NOTES: _____

_____
_____
_____
_____
_____
_____
_____
_____
_____
_____
_____

FAVORITE VERSE:
_____
_____
_____
_____

Today's Date & Time:

___ / ___ / ____   ____ : ____

Bible Passages Read:

_____
_____
_____

Prayer Concerns & Praise:

_____
_____
_____
_____
_____

NOTES:

_____
_____
_____
_____
_____
_____
_____
_____
_____

FAVORITE VERSE:

_____
_____
_____

Today's Date & Time:

____ / ____ / _____   ____ : ____

Bible Passages Read:

_____
_____
_____

Prayer Concerns & Praise:

_____
_____
_____
_____
_____

NOTES:

_____
_____
_____
_____
_____
_____
_____
_____
_____

FAVORITE VERSE:

_____
_____
_____

Today's Date & Time:

____ / ____ / _____   ____ : ____

Bible Passages Read:

_____
_____
_____

Prayer Concerns & Praise:

_____
_____
_____
_____
_____

NOTES:

FAVORITE VERSE:

Today's Date & Time:

___ / ___ / ___   ___ : ___

Bible Passages Read:

Prayer Concerns & Praise:

NOTES:

FAVORITE VERSE:

Today's Date & Time:

___ / ___ / ___   ___ : ___

Bible Passages Read:

Prayer Concerns & Praise:

NOTES:

_____

_____

_____

_____

_____

_____

_____

_____

_____

_____

_____

_____

FAVORITE VERSE:

_____

_____

_____

Today's Date & Time:

____ / ____ / ____   ____ : ____

Bible Passages Read:

_____

_____

Prayer Concerns & Praise:

_____

_____

_____

_____

_____

NOTES:

_____

_____

_____

_____

_____

_____

_____

_____

_____

_____

_____

_____

FAVORITE VERSE:

_____

_____

_____

Today's Date & Time:

____ / ____ / ____   ____ : ____

Bible Passages Read:

_____

_____

Prayer Concerns & Praise:

_____

_____

_____

_____

NOTES:

FAVORITE VERSE:

Today's Date & Time:

____ / ____ / _____ ____ : ____

Bible Passages Read:

Prayer Concerns & Praise:

NOTES:

FAVORITE VERSE:

Today's Date & Time:

____ / ____ / _____ ____ : ____

Bible Passages Read:

Prayer Concerns & Praise:

NOTES:

FAVORITE VERSE:

Today's Date & Time:

____ / ____ / _____   ____ : ____

Bible Passages Read:

Prayer Concerns & Praise:

NOTES:

FAVORITE VERSE:

Today's Date & Time:

____ / ____ / _____   ____ : ____

Bible Passages Read:

Prayer Concerns & Praise:

NOTES: _____

_____
_____
_____
_____
_____
_____
_____
_____
_____
_____

FAVORITE VERSE:

_____
_____
_____
_____

Today's Date & Time:

____ / ____ / _____   ____ : ____

Bible Passages Read:

_____
_____
_____

Prayer Concerns & Praise:

_____
_____
_____
_____
_____

NOTES: _____

_____
_____
_____
_____
_____
_____
_____
_____
_____
_____
_____

FAVORITE VERSE:

_____
_____
_____
_____

Today's Date & Time:

____ / ____ / _____   ____ : ____

Bible Passages Read:

_____
_____
_____

Prayer Concerns & Praise:

_____
_____
_____
_____
_____

NOTES: _____

_____

_____

_____

_____

_____

_____

_____

_____

_____

_____

FAVORITE VERSE:

_____

_____

_____

Today's Date & Time:

____ / ____ / _____   ____ : ____

Bible Passages Read:

_____

_____

Prayer Concerns & Praise:

_____

_____

_____

_____

_____

_____

NOTES: _____

_____

_____

_____

_____

_____

_____

_____

_____

_____

_____

FAVORITE VERSE:

_____

_____

_____

Today's Date & Time:

____ / ____ / _____   ____ : ____

Bible Passages Read:

_____

_____

Prayer Concerns & Praise:

_____

_____

_____

_____

_____

_____

NOTES: _____

_____
_____
_____
_____
_____
_____
_____
_____
_____
_____

FAVORITE VERSE:

_____
_____
_____
_____

Today's Date & Time:

____ / ____ / _____   ____ : ____

Bible Passages Read:

_____
_____

Prayer Concerns & Praise:

_____
_____
_____
_____
_____

NOTES: _____

_____
_____
_____
_____
_____
_____
_____
_____
_____
_____

FAVORITE VERSE:

_____
_____
_____
_____

Today's Date & Time:

____ / ____ / _____   ____ : ____

Bible Passages Read:

_____
_____

Prayer Concerns & Praise:

_____
_____
_____
_____
_____

NOTES:

_____
_____
_____
_____
_____
_____
_____
_____
_____
_____

FAVORITE VERSE:

_____
_____
_____

Today's Date & Time:

____ / ____ / ____   ____ : ____

Bible Passages Read:

_____
_____

Prayer Concerns & Praise:

_____
_____
_____
_____
_____

NOTES:

_____
_____
_____
_____
_____
_____
_____
_____
_____
_____

FAVORITE VERSE:

_____
_____
_____

Today's Date & Time:

____ / ____ / ____   ____ : ____

Bible Passages Read:

_____
_____

Prayer Concerns & Praise:

_____
_____
_____
_____
_____

NOTES:

_____

_____

_____

_____

_____

_____

_____

_____

_____

_____

FAVORITE VERSE:

_____

_____

_____

Today's Date & Time:

_____ / _____ / _____   _____ : _____

Bible Passages Read:

_____

_____

_____

Prayer Concerns & Praise:

_____

_____

_____

_____

_____

NOTES:

_____

_____

_____

_____

_____

_____

_____

_____

_____

_____

_____

FAVORITE VERSE:

_____

_____

_____

Today's Date & Time:

_____ / _____ / _____   _____ : _____

Bible Passages Read:

_____

_____

_____

Prayer Concerns & Praise:

_____

_____

_____

_____

_____

NOTES:

FAVORITE VERSE:

Today's Date & Time:

_____ / _____ / _____   _____ : _____

Bible Passages Read:

Prayer Concerns & Praise:

NOTES:

FAVORITE VERSE:

Today's Date & Time:

_____ / _____ / _____   _____ : _____

Bible Passages Read:

Prayer Concerns & Praise:

NOTES: _____

_____

_____

_____

_____

_____

_____

_____

_____

_____

_____

FAVORITE VERSE:

_____

_____

_____

Today's Date & Time:

____ / ____ / _____   ____ : ____

Bible Passages Read:

_____

_____

Prayer Concerns & Praise:

_____

_____

_____

_____

_____

NOTES: _____

_____

_____

_____

_____

_____

_____

_____

_____

_____

_____

FAVORITE VERSE:

_____

_____

_____

Today's Date & Time:

____ / ____ / _____   ____ : ____

Bible Passages Read:

_____

_____

Prayer Concerns & Praise:

_____

_____

_____

_____

_____

NOTES:

FAVORITE VERSE:

Today's Date & Time:

___ / ___ / _____   ___ : ___

Bible Passages Read:

Prayer Concerns & Praise:

NOTES:

FAVORITE VERSE:

Today's Date & Time:

___ / ___ / _____   ___ : ___

Bible Passages Read:

Prayer Concerns & Praise:

NOTES:

FAVORITE VERSE:

Today's Date & Time:

____ / ____ / ____   ____ : ____

Bible Passages Read:

Prayer Concerns & Praise:

NOTES:

FAVORITE VERSE:

Today's Date & Time:

____ / ____ / ____   ____ : ____

Bible Passages Read:

Prayer Concerns & Praise:

NOTES:

_____

_____

_____

_____

_____

_____

_____

_____

_____

_____

_____

FAVORITE VERSE:

_____

_____

_____

Today's Date & Time:

____ / ____ / _____   ____ : _____

Bible Passages Read:

_____

_____

_____

Prayer Concerns & Praise:

_____

_____

_____

_____

_____

_____

NOTES:

_____

_____

_____

_____

_____

_____

_____

_____

_____

_____

_____

FAVORITE VERSE:

_____

_____

_____

Today's Date & Time:

____ / ____ / _____   ____ : _____

Bible Passages Read:

_____

_____

_____

Prayer Concerns & Praise:

_____

_____

_____

_____

_____

NOTES:

FAVORITE VERSE:

Today's Date & Time:

____ / ____ / ____   ____ : ____

Bible Passages Read:

Prayer Concerns & Praise:

NOTES:

FAVORITE VERSE:

Today's Date & Time:

____ / ____ / ____   ____ : ____

Bible Passages Read:

Prayer Concerns & Praise:

NOTES:

FAVORITE VERSE:

Today's Date & Time:

____ / ____ / ____   ____ : ____

Bible Passages Read:

Prayer Concerns & Praise:

NOTES:

FAVORITE VERSE:

Today's Date & Time:

____ / ____ / ____   ____ : ____

Bible Passages Read:

Prayer Concerns & Praise:

NOTES:

FAVORITE VERSE:

Today's Date & Time:

____ / ____ / ____   ____ : ____

Bible Passages Read:

Prayer Concerns & Praise:

NOTES:

FAVORITE VERSE:

Today's Date & Time:

____ / ____ / ____   ____ : ____

Bible Passages Read:

Prayer Concerns & Praise:

NOTES:

_____

_____

_____

_____

_____

_____

_____

_____

_____

_____

_____

_____

FAVORITE VERSE:

_____

_____

_____

Today's Date & Time:

____ / ____ / ____   ____ : ____

Bible Passages Read:

_____

_____

Prayer Concerns & Praise:

_____

_____

_____

_____

_____

NOTES:

_____

_____

_____

_____

_____

_____

_____

_____

_____

_____

_____

_____

FAVORITE VERSE:

_____

_____

_____

Today's Date & Time:

____ / ____ / ____   ____ : ____

Bible Passages Read:

_____

_____

Prayer Concerns & Praise:

_____

_____

_____

_____

_____

NOTES: _____

_____
_____
_____
_____
_____
_____
_____
_____
_____
_____
_____

FAVORITE VERSE:
_____
_____
_____

Today's Date & Time:

____ / ____ / ____   ____ : ____

Bible Passages Read:

_____
_____

Prayer Concerns & Praise:

_____
_____
_____
_____
_____

NOTES: _____

_____
_____
_____
_____
_____
_____
_____
_____
_____
_____
_____

FAVORITE VERSE:
_____
_____
_____

Today's Date & Time:

____ / ____ / ____   ____ : ____

Bible Passages Read:

_____
_____

Prayer Concerns & Praise:

_____
_____
_____
_____
_____

NOTES:

_____

_____

_____

_____

_____

_____

_____

_____

_____

_____

_____

_____

FAVORITE VERSE:

_____

_____

_____

_____

Today's Date & Time:

____ / ____ / _____   ____ : ____

Bible Passages Read:

_____

_____

_____

Prayer Concerns & Praise:

_____

_____

_____

_____

_____

_____

NOTES:

_____

_____

_____

_____

_____

_____

_____

_____

_____

_____

_____

_____

FAVORITE VERSE:

_____

_____

_____

Today's Date & Time:

____ / ____ / _____   ____ : ____

Bible Passages Read:

_____

_____

_____

Prayer Concerns & Praise:

_____

_____

_____

_____

_____

NOTES:

FAVORITE VERSE:

Today's Date & Time:

____ / ____ / ____   ____ : ____

Bible Passages Read:

Prayer Concerns & Praise:

NOTES:

FAVORITE VERSE:

Today's Date & Time:

____ / ____ / ____   ____ : ____

Bible Passages Read:

Prayer Concerns & Praise:

NOTES:

FAVORITE VERSE:

Today's Date & Time:

____ / ____ / ____   ____ : ____

Bible Passages Read:

Prayer Concerns & Praise:

NOTES:

FAVORITE VERSE:

Today's Date & Time:

____ / ____ / ____   ____ : ____

Bible Passages Read:

Prayer Concerns & Praise:

NOTES:

FAVORITE VERSE:

Today's Date & Time:

____ / ____ / ____   ____ : ____

Bible Passages Read:

Prayer Concerns & Praise:

NOTES:

FAVORITE VERSE:

Today's Date & Time:

____ / ____ / ____   ____ : ____

Bible Passages Read:

Prayer Concerns & Praise:

NOTES:

FAVORITE VERSE:

Today's Date & Time:

____ / ____ / _____   ____ : ____

Bible Passages Read:

Prayer Concerns & Praise:

NOTES:

FAVORITE VERSE:

Today's Date & Time:

____ / ____ / _____   ____ : ____

Bible Passages Read:

Prayer Concerns & Praise:

NOTES: _____
_____
_____
_____
_____
_____
_____
_____
_____
_____
_____

FAVORITE VERSE:
_____
_____
_____
_____

Today's Date & Time:

____ / ____ / ____   ____ : ____

Bible Passages Read:
_____
_____
_____

Prayer Concerns & Praise:
_____
_____
_____
_____
_____
_____

NOTES: _____
_____
_____
_____
_____
_____
_____
_____
_____
_____
_____
_____

FAVORITE VERSE:
_____
_____
_____

Today's Date & Time:

____ / ____ / ____   ____ : ____

Bible Passages Read:
_____
_____
_____

Prayer Concerns & Praise:
_____
_____
_____
_____
_____
_____

NOTES:

FAVORITE VERSE:

Today's Date & Time:

____ / ____ / ____   ____ : ____

Bible Passages Read:

Prayer Concerns & Praise:

NOTES:

FAVORITE VERSE:

Today's Date & Time:

____ / ____ / ____   ____ : ____

Bible Passages Read:

Prayer Concerns & Praise:

NOTES:

FAVORITE VERSE:

Today's Date & Time:

_____ / _____ / _____   _____ : _____

Bible Passages Read:

Prayer Concerns & Praise:

NOTES:

FAVORITE VERSE:

Today's Date & Time:

_____ / _____ / _____   _____ : _____

Bible Passages Read:

Prayer Concerns & Praise:

NOTES:

FAVORITE VERSE:

Today's Date & Time:

____ / ____ / _____   ____ : ____

Bible Passages Read:

Prayer Concerns & Praise:

NOTES:

FAVORITE VERSE:

Today's Date & Time:

____ / ____ / _____   ____ : ____

Bible Passages Read:

Prayer Concerns & Praise:

NOTES:

FAVORITE VERSE:

Today's Date & Time:

____ / ____ / _____   _____ : ____

Bible Passages Read:

Prayer Concerns & Praise:

NOTES:

FAVORITE VERSE:

Today's Date & Time:

____ / ____ / _____   _____ : ____

Bible Passages Read:

Prayer Concerns & Praise:

NOTES:

FAVORITE VERSE:

Today's Date & Time:

____ / ____ / ____   ____ : ____

Bible Passages Read:

Prayer Concerns & Praise:

NOTES:

FAVORITE VERSE:

Today's Date & Time:

____ / ____ / ____   ____ : ____

Bible Passages Read:

Prayer Concerns & Praise:

NOTES:

FAVORITE VERSE:

Today's Date & Time:

___ / ___ / _____   ____ : ____

Bible Passages Read:

Prayer Concerns & Praise:

NOTES:

FAVORITE VERSE:

Today's Date & Time:

___ / ___ / _____   ____ : ____

Bible Passages Read:

Prayer Concerns & Praise:

NOTES: _____

_____

_____

_____

_____

_____

_____

_____

_____

_____

_____

FAVORITE VERSE: _____

_____

_____

_____

Today's Date & Time:

____ / ____ / _____   ____ : ____

Bible Passages Read:

_____

_____

_____

Prayer Concerns & Praise:

_____

_____

_____

_____

_____

_____

NOTES: _____

_____

_____

_____

_____

_____

_____

_____

_____

_____

_____

FAVORITE VERSE: _____

_____

_____

_____

Today's Date & Time:

____ / ____ / _____   ____ : ____

Bible Passages Read:

_____

_____

_____

Prayer Concerns & Praise:

_____

_____

_____

_____

_____

_____

NOTES:

FAVORITE VERSE:

Today's Date & Time:

____ / ____ / ____   ____ : ____

Bible Passages Read:

Prayer Concerns & Praise:

NOTES:

FAVORITE VERSE:

Today's Date & Time:

____ / ____ / ____   ____ : ____

Bible Passages Read:

Prayer Concerns & Praise:

NOTES:

FAVORITE VERSE:

Today's Date & Time:

____ / ____ / ____   ____ : ____

Bible Passages Read:

Prayer Concerns & Praise:

NOTES:

FAVORITE VERSE:

Today's Date & Time:

____ / ____ / ____   ____ : ____

Bible Passages Read:

Prayer Concerns & Praise:

NOTES:

_____

_____

_____

_____

_____

_____

_____

_____

_____

_____

_____

FAVORITE VERSE:

_____

_____

_____

Today's Date & Time:

____ / ____ / _____   ____ : ____

Bible Passages Read:

_____

_____

_____

Prayer Concerns & Praise:

_____

_____

_____

_____

_____

NOTES:

_____

_____

_____

_____

_____

_____

_____

_____

_____

_____

_____

FAVORITE VERSE:

_____

_____

_____

Today's Date & Time:

____ / ____ / _____   ____ : ____

Bible Passages Read:

_____

_____

_____

Prayer Concerns & Praise:

_____

_____

_____

_____

_____

NOTES: _____

_____
_____
_____
_____
_____
_____
_____
_____
_____
_____

FAVORITE VERSE:

_____
_____
_____

Today's Date & Time:

____ / ____ / _____   ____ : ____

Bible Passages Read:

_____
_____

Prayer Concerns & Praise:

_____
_____
_____
_____
_____

NOTES: _____

_____
_____
_____
_____
_____
_____
_____
_____
_____
_____

FAVORITE VERSE:

_____
_____
_____

Today's Date & Time:

____ / ____ / _____   ____ : ____

Bible Passages Read:

_____
_____

Prayer Concerns & Praise:

_____
_____
_____
_____
_____

NOTES:

_____

_____

_____

_____

_____

_____

_____

_____

_____

_____

_____

FAVORITE VERSE:

_____

_____

_____

Today's Date & Time:

_____ / _____ / _____   _____ : _____

Bible Passages Read:

_____

_____

_____

Prayer Concerns & Praise:

_____

_____

_____

_____

_____

NOTES:

_____

_____

_____

_____

_____

_____

_____

_____

_____

_____

_____

FAVORITE VERSE:

_____

_____

_____

Today's Date & Time:

_____ / _____ / _____   _____ : _____

Bible Passages Read:

_____

_____

_____

Prayer Concerns & Praise:

_____

_____

_____

_____

_____

NOTES:

FAVORITE VERSE:

Today's Date & Time:

_____ / _____ / _____   _____ : _____

Bible Passages Read:

Prayer Concerns & Praise:

NOTES:

FAVORITE VERSE:

Today's Date & Time:

_____ / _____ / _____   _____ : _____

Bible Passages Read:

Prayer Concerns & Praise:

NOTES: _____

_____

_____

_____

_____

_____

_____

_____

_____

_____

_____

FAVORITE VERSE: _____

_____

_____

_____

Today's Date & Time:

____ / ____ / ____   ____ : ____

Bible Passages Read:

_____

_____

_____

Prayer Concerns & Praise:

_____

_____

_____

_____

_____

NOTES: _____

_____

_____

_____

_____

_____

_____

_____

_____

_____

_____

FAVORITE VERSE: _____

_____

_____

_____

Today's Date & Time:

____ / ____ / ____   ____ : ____

Bible Passages Read:

_____

_____

_____

Prayer Concerns & Praise:

_____

_____

_____

_____

_____

NOTES:

FAVORITE VERSE:

Today's Date & Time:

_____ / _____ / _____   _____ : _____

Bible Passages Read:

Prayer Concerns & Praise:

NOTES:

FAVORITE VERSE:

Today's Date & Time:

_____ / _____ / _____   _____ : _____

Bible Passages Read:

Prayer Concerns & Praise:

NOTES:

FAVORITE VERSE:

Today's Date & Time:

____ / ____ / _____   ____ : ____

Bible Passages Read:

Prayer Concerns & Praise:

NOTES:

FAVORITE VERSE:

Today's Date & Time:

____ / ____ / _____   ____ : ____

Bible Passages Read:

Prayer Concerns & Praise:

NOTES: _____

_____
_____
_____
_____
_____
_____
_____
_____
_____
_____
_____

FAVORITE VERSE: _____

_____
_____
_____
_____

Today's Date & Time:

____ / ____ / ____   ____ : ____

Bible Passages Read:

_____
_____
_____

Prayer Concerns & Praise:

_____
_____
_____
_____
_____
_____

NOTES: _____

_____
_____
_____
_____
_____
_____
_____
_____
_____
_____
_____

FAVORITE VERSE: _____

_____
_____
_____
_____

Today's Date & Time:

____ / ____ / ____   ____ : ____

Bible Passages Read:

_____
_____
_____

Prayer Concerns & Praise:

_____
_____
_____
_____
_____
_____

NOTES: _____

_____
_____
_____
_____
_____
_____
_____
_____
_____
_____
_____

FAVORITE VERSE: _____

_____
_____
_____

Today's Date & Time:

____ / ____ / _____   ____ : ____

Bible Passages Read:

_____
_____
_____

Prayer Concerns & Praise:

_____
_____
_____
_____
_____

NOTES: _____

_____
_____
_____
_____
_____
_____
_____
_____
_____
_____
_____

FAVORITE VERSE: _____

_____
_____
_____

Today's Date & Time:

____ / ____ / _____   ____ : ____

Bible Passages Read:

_____
_____
_____

Prayer Concerns & Praise:

_____
_____
_____
_____
_____

NOTES:

FAVORITE VERSE:

Today's Date & Time:

____ / ____ / _____   ____ : ____

Bible Passages Read:

Prayer Concerns & Praise:

NOTES:

FAVORITE VERSE:

Today's Date & Time:

____ / ____ / _____   ____ : ____

Bible Passages Read:

Prayer Concerns & Praise:

NOTES:

FAVORITE VERSE:

Today's Date & Time:

_____ / _____ / _____   _____ : _____

Bible Passages Read:

Prayer Concerns & Praise:

NOTES:

FAVORITE VERSE:

Today's Date & Time:

_____ / _____ / _____   _____ : _____

Bible Passages Read:

Prayer Concerns & Praise:

NOTES: _____

_____
_____
_____
_____
_____
_____
_____
_____
_____
_____
_____

FAVORITE VERSE:

_____
_____
_____
_____

Today's Date & Time:

____ / ____ / ____   ____ : ____

Bible Passages Read:

_____
_____
_____

Prayer Concerns & Praise:

_____
_____
_____
_____
_____
_____

NOTES: _____

_____
_____
_____
_____
_____
_____
_____
_____
_____
_____
_____

FAVORITE VERSE:

_____
_____
_____
_____

Today's Date & Time:

____ / ____ / ____   ____ : ____

Bible Passages Read:

_____
_____
_____

Prayer Concerns & Praise:

_____
_____
_____
_____
_____
_____

NOTES: _____

_____
_____
_____
_____
_____
_____
_____
_____
_____
_____

FAVORITE VERSE: _____

_____
_____
_____

Today's Date & Time:

____ / ____ / _____   ____ : ____

Bible Passages Read:

_____
_____

Prayer Concerns & Praise:

_____
_____
_____
_____
_____

NOTES: _____

_____
_____
_____
_____
_____
_____
_____
_____
_____
_____

FAVORITE VERSE: _____

_____
_____
_____

Today's Date & Time:

____ / ____ / _____   ____ : ____

Bible Passages Read:

_____
_____

Prayer Concerns & Praise:

_____
_____
_____
_____
_____

NOTES:

FAVORITE VERSE:

Today's Date & Time:

_____ / _____ / _____   _____ : _____

Bible Passages Read:

Prayer Concerns & Praise:

NOTES:

FAVORITE VERSE:

Today's Date & Time:

_____ / _____ / _____   _____ : _____

Bible Passages Read:

Prayer Concerns & Praise:

NOTES:

_____
_____
_____
_____
_____
_____
_____
_____
_____
_____
_____
_____

FAVORITE VERSE:

_____
_____
_____

Today's Date & Time:

____ / ____ / ____   ____ : ____

Bible Passages Read:

_____
_____
_____

Prayer Concerns & Praise:

_____
_____
_____
_____
_____

NOTES:

_____
_____
_____
_____
_____
_____
_____
_____
_____
_____
_____
_____

FAVORITE VERSE:

_____
_____
_____

Today's Date & Time:

____ / ____ / ____   ____ : ____

Bible Passages Read:

_____
_____
_____

Prayer Concerns & Praise:

_____
_____
_____
_____
_____

NOTES:

_____
_____
_____
_____
_____
_____
_____
_____
_____
_____
_____

FAVORITE VERSE:

_____
_____
_____
_____

Today's Date & Time:

____ / ____ / ____   ____ : ____

Bible Passages Read:

_____
_____
_____

Prayer Concerns & Praise:

_____
_____
_____
_____
_____
_____

NOTES:

_____
_____
_____
_____
_____
_____
_____
_____
_____
_____
_____

FAVORITE VERSE:

_____
_____
_____
_____

Today's Date & Time:

____ / ____ / ____   ____ : ____

Bible Passages Read:

_____
_____
_____

Prayer Concerns & Praise:

_____
_____
_____
_____
_____

NOTES:

FAVORITE VERSE:

Today's Date & Time:

____ / ____ / ____   ____ : ____

Bible Passages Read:

Prayer Concerns & Praise:

NOTES:

FAVORITE VERSE:

Today's Date & Time:

____ / ____ / ____   ____ : ____

Bible Passages Read:

Prayer Concerns & Praise:

NOTES:

FAVORITE VERSE:

Today's Date & Time:

____ / ____ / _____   ____ : ____

Bible Passages Read:

Prayer Concerns & Praise:

NOTES:

FAVORITE VERSE:

Today's Date & Time:

____ / ____ / _____   ____ : ____

Bible Passages Read:

Prayer Concerns & Praise:

NOTES: _____

_____

_____

_____

_____

_____

_____

_____

_____

_____

_____

FAVORITE VERSE:

_____

_____

_____

Today's Date & Time:

____ / ____ / _____   ____ : ____

Bible Passages Read:

_____

_____

_____

Prayer Concerns & Praise:

_____

_____

_____

_____

_____

NOTES: _____

_____

_____

_____

_____

_____

_____

_____

_____

_____

_____

FAVORITE VERSE:

_____

_____

_____

Today's Date & Time:

____ / ____ / _____   ____ : ____

Bible Passages Read:

_____

_____

_____

Prayer Concerns & Praise:

_____

_____

_____

_____

NOTES:

FAVORITE VERSE:

Today's Date & Time:

____ / ____ / ____   ____ : ____

Bible Passages Read:

Prayer Concerns & Praise:

NOTES:

FAVORITE VERSE:

Today's Date & Time:

____ / ____ / ____   ____ : ____

Bible Passages Read:

Prayer Concerns & Praise:

NOTES: _____

_____
_____
_____
_____
_____
_____
_____
_____
_____
_____
_____

FAVORITE VERSE:

_____
_____
_____
_____

Today's Date & Time:

_____ / _____ / _____   _____ : _____

Bible Passages Read:

_____
_____

Prayer Concerns & Praise:

_____
_____
_____
_____
_____

NOTES: _____

_____
_____
_____
_____
_____
_____
_____
_____
_____

FAVORITE VERSE:

_____
_____
_____

Today's Date & Time:

_____ / _____ / _____   _____ : _____

Bible Passages Read:

_____
_____

Prayer Concerns & Praise:

_____
_____
_____
_____
_____

NOTES:

FAVORITE VERSE:

NOTES:

FAVORITE VERSE:

Today's Date & Time:

___ / ___ / ____   ____ : ____

Bible Passages Read:

Prayer Concerns & Praise:

Today's Date & Time:

___ / ___ / ____   ____ : ____

Bible Passages Read:

Prayer Concerns & Praise:

NOTES: _____

_____
_____
_____
_____
_____
_____
_____
_____
_____
_____
_____
_____

FAVORITE VERSE:

_____
_____
_____

Today's Date & Time:

____ / ____ / ____   ____ : ____

Bible Passages Read:

_____
_____

Prayer Concerns & Praise:

_____
_____
_____
_____

NOTES: _____

_____
_____
_____
_____
_____
_____
_____
_____
_____
_____
_____
_____

FAVORITE VERSE:

_____
_____
_____

Today's Date & Time:

____ / ____ / ____   ____ : ____

Bible Passages Read:

_____
_____

Prayer Concerns & Praise:

_____
_____
_____
_____

NOTES: _____

_____
_____
_____
_____
_____
_____
_____
_____
_____
_____
_____

FAVORITE VERSE:
_____
_____
_____

Today's Date & Time:

____ / ____ / ____   ____ : ____

Bible Passages Read:

_____
_____
_____

Prayer Concerns & Praise:

_____
_____
_____
_____
_____
_____

NOTES: _____

_____
_____
_____
_____
_____
_____
_____
_____
_____
_____
_____

FAVORITE VERSE:
_____
_____
_____

Today's Date & Time:

____ / ____ / ____   ____ : ____

Bible Passages Read:

_____
_____
_____

Prayer Concerns & Praise:

_____
_____
_____
_____
_____

NOTES:

FAVORITE VERSE:

Today's Date & Time:

_____ / _____ / _____   _____ : _____

Bible Passages Read:

Prayer Concerns & Praise:

NOTES:

FAVORITE VERSE:

Today's Date & Time:

_____ / _____ / _____   _____ : _____

Bible Passages Read:

Prayer Concerns & Praise:

NOTES:

FAVORITE VERSE:

Today's Date & Time:

____ / ____ / ____ ____ : ____

Bible Passages Read:

Prayer Concerns & Praise:

NOTES:

FAVORITE VERSE:

Today's Date & Time:

____ / ____ / ____ ____ : ____

Bible Passages Read:

Prayer Concerns & Praise:

NOTES:

FAVORITE VERSE:

____ / ____ / ____   ____ : ____

Bible Passages Read:

Prayer Concerns & Praise:

NOTES:

FAVORITE VERSE:

Today's Date & Time:

____ / ____ / ____   ____ : ____

Bible Passages Read:

Prayer Concerns & Praise:

NOTES: _____

_____

_____

_____

_____

_____

_____

_____

_____

_____

_____

_____

FAVORITE VERSE:

_____

_____

_____

Today's Date & Time:

____ / ____ / _____   ____ : ____

Bible Passages Read:

_____

_____

Prayer Concerns & Praise:

_____

_____

_____

_____

_____

NOTES: _____

_____

_____

_____

_____

_____

_____

_____

_____

_____

_____

_____

FAVORITE VERSE:

_____

_____

_____

Today's Date & Time:

____ / ____ / _____   ____ : ____

Bible Passages Read:

_____

_____

Prayer Concerns & Praise:

_____

_____

_____

_____

NOTES:

FAVORITE VERSE:

Today's Date & Time:

____ / ____ / _____   ____ : ____

Bible Passages Read:

Prayer Concerns & Praise:

NOTES:

FAVORITE VERSE:

Today's Date & Time:

____ / ____ / _____   ____ : ____

Bible Passages Read:

Prayer Concerns & Praise:

NOTES:

_____
_____
_____
_____
_____
_____
_____
_____
_____
_____

FAVORITE VERSE:

_____
_____
_____
_____

Today's Date & Time:

____ / ____ / ____   ____ : ____

Bible Passages Read:

_____
_____

Prayer Concerns & Praise:

_____
_____
_____
_____
_____

NOTES:

_____
_____
_____
_____
_____
_____
_____
_____
_____
_____

FAVORITE VERSE:

_____
_____
_____

Today's Date & Time:

____ / ____ / ____   ____ : ____

Bible Passages Read:

_____
_____

Prayer Concerns & Praise:

_____
_____
_____
_____

NOTES:

FAVORITE VERSE:

Today's Date & Time:

____ / ____ / ____   ____ : ____

Bible Passages Read:

Prayer Concerns & Praise:

NOTES:

FAVORITE VERSE:

Today's Date & Time:

____ / ____ / ____   ____ : ____

Bible Passages Read:

Prayer Concerns & Praise:

NOTES:

_____

_____

_____

_____

_____

_____

_____

_____

_____

_____

_____

_____

FAVORITE VERSE:

_____

_____

_____

Today's Date & Time:

_____ / _____ / _____   _____ : _____

Bible Passages Read:

_____

_____

_____

Prayer Concerns & Praise:

_____

_____

_____

_____

_____

_____

NOTES:

_____

_____

_____

_____

_____

_____

_____

_____

_____

_____

_____

_____

FAVORITE VERSE:

_____

_____

_____

Today's Date & Time:

_____ / _____ / _____   _____ : _____

Bible Passages Read:

_____

_____

_____

Prayer Concerns & Praise:

_____

_____

_____

_____

_____

NOTES:

FAVORITE VERSE:

Today's Date & Time:

____ / ____ / ____   ____ : ____

Bible Passages Read:

Prayer Concerns & Praise:

NOTES:

FAVORITE VERSE:

Today's Date & Time:

____ / ____ / ____   ____ : ____

Bible Passages Read:

Prayer Concerns & Praise:

NOTES: _____

_____
_____
_____
_____
_____
_____
_____
_____
_____
_____
_____

FAVORITE VERSE: _____

_____
_____
_____
_____

Today's Date & Time:

____ / ____ / ____   ____ : ____

Bible Passages Read:

_____
_____
_____

Prayer Concerns & Praise:

_____
_____
_____
_____
_____
_____

NOTES: _____

_____
_____
_____
_____
_____
_____
_____
_____
_____
_____
_____

FAVORITE VERSE: _____

_____
_____
_____
_____

Today's Date & Time:

____ / ____ / ____   ____ : ____

Bible Passages Read:

_____
_____
_____

Prayer Concerns & Praise:

_____
_____
_____
_____
_____
_____

NOTES: _____

_____

_____

_____

_____

_____

_____

_____

_____

_____

_____

FAVORITE VERSE: _____

_____

_____

_____

Today's Date & Time:

____ / ____ / ____   ____ : ____

Bible Passages Read:

_____

_____

_____

Prayer Concerns & Praise:

_____

_____

_____

_____

_____

NOTES: _____

_____

_____

_____

_____

_____

_____

_____

_____

_____

_____

_____

FAVORITE VERSE: _____

_____

_____

_____

Today's Date & Time:

____ / ____ / ____   ____ : ____

Bible Passages Read:

_____

_____

_____

Prayer Concerns & Praise:

_____

_____

_____

_____

_____

NOTES:

FAVORITE VERSE:

NOTES:

FAVORITE VERSE:

Today's Date & Time:

____ / ____ / ____   ____ : ____

Bible Passages Read:

Prayer Concerns & Praise:

Today's Date & Time:

____ / ____ / ____   ____ : ____

Bible Passages Read:

Prayer Concerns & Praise:

NOTES:

FAVORITE VERSE:

Today's Date & Time:

____ / ____ / ____   ____ : ____

Bible Passages Read:

Prayer Concerns & Praise:

NOTES:

FAVORITE VERSE:

Today's Date & Time:

____ / ____ / ____   ____ : ____

Bible Passages Read:

Prayer Concerns & Praise:

NOTES: _____

_____
_____
_____
_____
_____
_____
_____
_____
_____
_____
_____

FAVORITE VERSE:

_____
_____
_____

Today's Date & Time:

____ / ____ / _____   ____ : ____

Bible Passages Read:

_____
_____
_____

Prayer Concerns & Praise:

_____
_____
_____
_____
_____
_____

NOTES: _____

_____
_____
_____
_____
_____
_____
_____
_____
_____
_____
_____
_____

FAVORITE VERSE:

_____
_____
_____

Today's Date & Time:

____ / ____ / _____   ____ : ____

Bible Passages Read:

_____
_____
_____

Prayer Concerns & Praise:

_____
_____
_____
_____
_____
_____

NOTES: _____

_____
_____
_____
_____
_____
_____
_____
_____
_____
_____
_____

FAVORITE VERSE:

_____
_____
_____

Today's Date & Time:

____ / ____ / _____   ____ : ____

Bible Passages Read:

_____
_____
_____

Prayer Concerns & Praise:

_____
_____
_____
_____
_____
_____

NOTES: _____

_____
_____
_____
_____
_____
_____
_____
_____
_____
_____
_____

FAVORITE VERSE:

_____
_____
_____

Today's Date & Time:

____ / ____ / _____   ____ : ____

Bible Passages Read:

_____
_____
_____

Prayer Concerns & Praise:

_____
_____
_____
_____
_____

NOTES:

FAVORITE VERSE:

Today's Date & Time:

____ / ____ / ____   ____ : ____

Bible Passages Read:

Prayer Concerns & Praise:

NOTES:

FAVORITE VERSE:

Today's Date & Time:

____ / ____ / ____   ____ : ____

Bible Passages Read:

Prayer Concerns & Praise:

NOTES: _____

_____
_____
_____
_____
_____
_____
_____
_____
_____
_____
_____

FAVORITE VERSE: _____

_____
_____
_____

Today's Date & Time:

____ / ____ / ____   ____ : ____

Bible Passages Read:

_____
_____
_____

Prayer Concerns & Praise:

_____
_____
_____
_____
_____
_____

NOTES: _____

_____
_____
_____
_____
_____
_____
_____
_____
_____
_____
_____

FAVORITE VERSE: _____

_____
_____
_____

Today's Date & Time:

____ / ____ / ____   ____ : ____

Bible Passages Read:

_____
_____
_____

Prayer Concerns & Praise:

_____
_____
_____
_____
_____
_____

NOTES:

FAVORITE VERSE:

Today's Date & Time:

____ / ____ / ____   ____ : ____

Bible Passages Read:

Prayer Concerns & Praise:

NOTES:

FAVORITE VERSE:

Today's Date & Time:

____ / ____ / ____   ____ : ____

Bible Passages Read:

Prayer Concerns & Praise:

NOTES: _____

_____

_____

_____

_____

_____

_____

_____

_____

_____

_____

_____

FAVORITE VERSE: _____

_____

_____

_____

Today's Date & Time:

____ / ____ / ____   ____ : ____

Bible Passages Read:

_____

_____

_____

Prayer Concerns & Praise:

_____

_____

_____

_____

_____

_____

NOTES: _____

_____

_____

_____

_____

_____

_____

_____

_____

_____

_____

_____

_____

_____

FAVORITE VERSE: _____

_____

_____

_____

Today's Date & Time:

____ / ____ / ____   ____ : ____

Bible Passages Read:

_____

_____

_____

Prayer Concerns & Praise:

_____

_____

_____

_____

_____

_____

NOTES:

FAVORITE VERSE:

Today's Date & Time:

____ / ____ / ____   ____ : ____

Bible Passages Read:

Prayer Concerns & Praise:

NOTES:

FAVORITE VERSE:

Today's Date & Time:

____ / ____ / ____   ____ : ____

Bible Passages Read:

Prayer Concerns & Praise:

NOTES: _____

_____
_____
_____
_____
_____
_____
_____
_____
_____
_____
_____

FAVORITE VERSE: _____

_____
_____
_____

Today's Date & Time:

____ / ____ / ____   ____ : ____

Bible Passages Read:

_____
_____
_____

Prayer Concerns & Praise:

_____
_____
_____
_____
_____

NOTES: _____

_____
_____
_____
_____
_____
_____
_____
_____
_____

FAVORITE VERSE: _____

_____
_____
_____

Today's Date & Time:

____ / ____ / ____   ____ : ____

Bible Passages Read:

_____
_____
_____

Prayer Concerns & Praise:

_____
_____
_____
_____
_____

NOTES:

FAVORITE VERSE:

Today's Date & Time:

____ / ____ / ____   ____ : ____

Bible Passages Read:

Prayer Concerns & Praise:

NOTES:

FAVORITE VERSE:

Today's Date & Time:

____ / ____ / ____   ____ : ____

Bible Passages Read:

Prayer Concerns & Praise:

NOTES:

FAVORITE VERSE:

Today's Date & Time:

____ / ____ / ____   ____ : ____

Bible Passages Read:

Prayer Concerns & Praise:

NOTES:

FAVORITE VERSE:

Today's Date & Time:

____ / ____ / ____   ____ : ____

Bible Passages Read:

Prayer Concerns & Praise:

NOTES: _____

_____

_____

_____

_____

_____

_____

_____

_____

_____

_____

_____

FAVORITE VERSE:

_____

_____

_____

_____

Today's Date & Time:

____ / ____ / ____   ____ : ____

Bible Passages Read:

_____

_____

_____

Prayer Concerns & Praise:

_____

_____

_____

_____

_____

_____

NOTES: _____

_____

_____

_____

_____

_____

_____

_____

_____

_____

_____

_____

FAVORITE VERSE:

_____

_____

_____

_____

Today's Date & Time:

____ / ____ / ____   ____ : ____

Bible Passages Read:

_____

_____

_____

Prayer Concerns & Praise:

_____

_____

_____

_____

_____

_____

NOTES: _____

_____
_____
_____
_____
_____
_____
_____
_____
_____
_____
_____

FAVORITE VERSE: _____

_____
_____
_____

Today's Date & Time:

____ / ____ / ____   ____ : ____

Bible Passages Read:

_____
_____
_____

Prayer Concerns & Praise:

_____
_____
_____
_____
_____

NOTES: _____

_____
_____
_____
_____
_____
_____
_____
_____
_____
_____
_____
_____

FAVORITE VERSE: _____

_____
_____
_____

Today's Date & Time:

____ / ____ / ____   ____ : ____

Bible Passages Read:

_____
_____
_____

Prayer Concerns & Praise:

_____
_____
_____
_____
_____

NOTES:

FAVORITE VERSE:

Today's Date & Time:

____ / ____ / ____   ____ : ____

Bible Passages Read:

Prayer Concerns & Praise:

NOTES:

FAVORITE VERSE:

Today's Date & Time:

____ / ____ / ____   ____ : ____

Bible Passages Read:

Prayer Concerns & Praise:

NOTES: _____

_____
_____
_____
_____
_____
_____
_____
_____
_____
_____
_____
_____

FAVORITE VERSE:

_____
_____
_____

Today's Date & Time:

____ / ____ / ____   ____ : ____

Bible Passages Read:

_____
_____
_____

Prayer Concerns & Praise:

_____
_____
_____
_____
_____
_____

NOTES: _____

_____
_____
_____
_____
_____
_____
_____
_____
_____
_____
_____
_____

FAVORITE VERSE:

_____
_____
_____

Today's Date & Time:

____ / ____ / ____   ____ : ____

Bible Passages Read:

_____
_____
_____

Prayer Concerns & Praise:

_____
_____
_____
_____
_____
_____

NOTES:

FAVORITE VERSE:

Today's Date & Time:

____ / ____ / ____   ____ : ____

Bible Passages Read:

Prayer Concerns & Praise:

NOTES:

FAVORITE VERSE:

Today's Date & Time:

____ / ____ / ____   ____ : ____

Bible Passages Read:

Prayer Concerns & Praise:

NOTES: _____

_____
_____
_____
_____
_____
_____
_____
_____
_____
_____
_____

FAVORITE VERSE:

_____
_____
_____

Today's Date & Time:

____ / ____ / ____   ____ : ____

Bible Passages Read:

_____
_____
_____

Prayer Concerns & Praise:

_____
_____
_____
_____
_____
_____

NOTES: _____

_____
_____
_____
_____
_____
_____
_____
_____
_____
_____
_____

FAVORITE VERSE:

_____
_____
_____

Today's Date & Time:

____ / ____ / ____   ____ : ____

Bible Passages Read:

_____
_____
_____

Prayer Concerns & Praise:

_____
_____
_____
_____
_____
_____

NOTES:

_____
_____
_____
_____
_____
_____
_____
_____
_____
_____

FAVORITE VERSE:

_____
_____
_____

Today's Date & Time:

____ / ____ / _____   ____ : ____

Bible Passages Read:

_____
_____

Prayer Concerns & Praise:

_____
_____
_____
_____
_____

NOTES:

_____
_____
_____
_____
_____
_____
_____
_____
_____
_____

FAVORITE VERSE:

_____
_____
_____

Today's Date & Time:

____ / ____ / _____   ____ : ____

Bible Passages Read:

_____
_____

Prayer Concerns & Praise:

_____
_____
_____
_____
_____

NOTES:

FAVORITE VERSE:

Today's Date & Time:

____ / ____ / _____   ____ : ____

Bible Passages Read:

Prayer Concerns & Praise:

NOTES:

FAVORITE VERSE:

Today's Date & Time:

____ / ____ / _____   ____ : ____

Bible Passages Read:

Prayer Concerns & Praise:

NOTES: _____

_____
_____
_____
_____
_____
_____
_____
_____
_____
_____

FAVORITE VERSE:
_____
_____
_____
_____

Today's Date & Time:

____ / ____ / _____   ____ : ____

Bible Passages Read:

_____
_____
_____

Prayer Concerns & Praise:

_____
_____
_____
_____
_____

NOTES: _____

_____
_____
_____
_____
_____
_____
_____
_____
_____
_____

FAVORITE VERSE:
_____
_____
_____
_____

Today's Date & Time:

____ / ____ / _____   ____ : ____

Bible Passages Read:

_____
_____
_____

Prayer Concerns & Praise:

_____
_____
_____
_____

NOTES:

FAVORITE VERSE:

Today's Date & Time:

____ / ____ / ____   ____ : ____

Bible Passages Read:

Prayer Concerns & Praise:

NOTES:

FAVORITE VERSE:

Today's Date & Time:

____ / ____ / ____   ____ : ____

Bible Passages Read:

Prayer Concerns & Praise:

NOTES:

FAVORITE VERSE:

Today's Date & Time:

____ / ____ / ____   ____ : ____

Bible Passages Read:

Prayer Concerns & Praise:

NOTES:

FAVORITE VERSE:

Today's Date & Time:

____ / ____ / ____   ____ : ____

Bible Passages Read:

Prayer Concerns & Praise:

NOTES:

FAVORITE VERSE:

Today's Date & Time:

___ / ___ / ____   ____ : ____

Bible Passages Read:

Prayer Concerns & Praise:

NOTES:

FAVORITE VERSE:

Today's Date & Time:

___ / ___ / ____   ____ : ____

Bible Passages Read:

Prayer Concerns & Praise:

NOTES:

FAVORITE VERSE:

Today's Date & Time:

____ / ____ / ____   ____ : ____

Bible Passages Read:

Prayer Concerns & Praise:

NOTES:

FAVORITE VERSE:

Today's Date & Time:

____ / ____ / ____   ____ : ____

Bible Passages Read:

Prayer Concerns & Praise:

NOTES: _____

_____
_____
_____
_____
_____
_____
_____
_____
_____
_____

FAVORITE VERSE:
_____
_____
_____
_____

Today's Date & Time:

____ / ____ / ____   ____ : ____

Bible Passages Read:

_____
_____
_____

Prayer Concerns & Praise:

_____
_____
_____
_____
_____

NOTES: _____

_____
_____
_____
_____
_____
_____
_____
_____
_____
_____
_____

FAVORITE VERSE:
_____
_____
_____
_____

Today's Date & Time:

____ / ____ / ____   ____ : ____

Bible Passages Read:

_____
_____
_____

Prayer Concerns & Praise:

_____
_____
_____
_____

NOTES: _____

_____
_____
_____
_____
_____
_____
_____
_____
_____
_____
_____

FAVORITE VERSE: _____

_____
_____
_____

Today's Date & Time:

____ / ____ / _____   ____ : ____

Bible Passages Read:

_____
_____
_____

Prayer Concerns & Praise:

_____
_____
_____
_____
_____
_____

NOTES: _____

_____
_____
_____
_____
_____
_____
_____
_____
_____
_____
_____

FAVORITE VERSE: _____

_____
_____
_____

Today's Date & Time:

____ / ____ / _____   ____ : ____

Bible Passages Read:

_____
_____
_____

Prayer Concerns & Praise:

_____
_____
_____
_____
_____
_____

NOTES:

FAVORITE VERSE:

Today's Date & Time:

____ / ____ / ____   ____ : ____

Bible Passages Read:

Prayer Concerns & Praise:

NOTES:

FAVORITE VERSE:

Today's Date & Time:

____ / ____ / ____   ____ : ____

Bible Passages Read:

Prayer Concerns & Praise:

NOTES:

FAVORITE VERSE:

Today's Date & Time:

____ / ____ / ____   ____ : ____

Bible Passages Read:

Prayer Concerns & Praise:

NOTES:

FAVORITE VERSE:

Today's Date & Time:

____ / ____ / ____   ____ : ____

Bible Passages Read:

Prayer Concerns & Praise:

NOTES: _____

_____

_____

_____

_____

_____

_____

_____

_____

_____

_____

FAVORITE VERSE:

_____

_____

_____

_____

Today's Date & Time:

____ / ____ / ____   ____ : ____

Bible Passages Read:

_____

_____

_____

Prayer Concerns & Praise:

_____

_____

_____

_____

_____

_____

NOTES: _____

_____

_____

_____

_____

_____

_____

_____

_____

_____

_____

_____

FAVORITE VERSE:

_____

_____

_____

_____

Today's Date & Time:

____ / ____ / ____   ____ : ____

Bible Passages Read:

_____

_____

_____

Prayer Concerns & Praise:

_____

_____

_____

_____

_____

_____

NOTES:

FAVORITE VERSE:

Today's Date & Time:

____ / ____ / ____   ____ : ____

Bible Passages Read:

Prayer Concerns & Praise:

NOTES:

FAVORITE VERSE:

Today's Date & Time:

____ / ____ / ____   ____ : ____

Bible Passages Read:

Prayer Concerns & Praise:

NOTES:

FAVORITE VERSE:

NOTES:

FAVORITE VERSE:

Today's Date & Time:

____ / ____ / ____   ____ : ____

Bible Passages Read:

Prayer Concerns & Praise:

Today's Date & Time:

____ / ____ / ____   ____ : ____

Bible Passages Read:

Prayer Concerns & Praise:

NOTES:

FAVORITE VERSE:

Today's Date & Time:

____ / ____ / ____   ____ : ____

Bible Passages Read:

Prayer Concerns & Praise:

NOTES:

FAVORITE VERSE:

Today's Date & Time:

____ / ____ / ____   ____ : ____

Bible Passages Read:

Prayer Concerns & Praise:

NOTES:

FAVORITE VERSE:

___ / ___ / _____   ___ : ___

Bible Passages Read:

Prayer Concerns & Praise:

NOTES:

FAVORITE VERSE:

Today's Date & Time:

___ / ___ / _____   ___ : ___

Bible Passages Read:

Prayer Concerns & Praise:

NOTES:

FAVORITE VERSE:

Today's Date & Time:

____ / ____ / ____   ____ : ____

Bible Passages Read:

Prayer Concerns & Praise:

NOTES:

FAVORITE VERSE:

Today's Date & Time:

____ / ____ / ____   ____ : ____

Bible Passages Read:

Prayer Concerns & Praise:

NOTES:

FAVORITE VERSE:

Today's Date & Time:

___ / ___ / _____   ___ : ___

Bible Passages Read:

Prayer Concerns & Praise:

NOTES:

FAVORITE VERSE:

Today's Date & Time:

___ / ___ / _____   ___ : ___

Bible Passages Read:

Prayer Concerns & Praise:

NOTES:

FAVORITE VERSE:

Today's Date & Time:

____ / ____ / ____   ____ : ____

Bible Passages Read:

Prayer Concerns & Praise:

NOTES:

FAVORITE VERSE:

Today's Date & Time:

____ / ____ / ____   ____ : ____

Bible Passages Read:

Prayer Concerns & Praise:

NOTES:

FAVORITE VERSE:

Today's Date & Time:

_____ / _____ / _____   _____ : _____

Bible Passages Read:

Prayer Concerns & Praise:

NOTES:

FAVORITE VERSE:

Today's Date & Time:

_____ / _____ / _____   _____ : _____

Bible Passages Read:

Prayer Concerns & Praise:

NOTES:

FAVORITE VERSE:

Today's Date & Time:

____ / ____ / ____   ____ : ____

Bible Passages Read:

Prayer Concerns & Praise:

NOTES:

FAVORITE VERSE:

Today's Date & Time:

____ / ____ / ____   ____ : ____

Bible Passages Read:

Prayer Concerns & Praise:

NOTES:

_____
_____
_____
_____
_____
_____
_____
_____
_____
_____
_____

FAVORITE VERSE:

_____
_____
_____

Today's Date & Time:

____ / ____ / ____   ____ : ____

Bible Passages Read:

_____
_____

Prayer Concerns & Praise:

_____
_____
_____
_____

NOTES:

_____
_____
_____
_____
_____
_____
_____
_____
_____
_____
_____

FAVORITE VERSE:

_____
_____
_____

Today's Date & Time:

____ / ____ / ____   ____ : ____

Bible Passages Read:

_____
_____

Prayer Concerns & Praise:

_____
_____
_____
_____

Final Thoughts:

To Work on for Next Year: